Good Beyond Evil:
Xunzi on human nature

Translated by Mingyuan Hu

Hermits United
London · Paris

Published in Great Britain by Hermits United Ltd. 2023
English translation copyright © Mingyuan Hu 2023
Printed in Europe

This book is part of the Erstwhile Series
A catalogue record for this book is available
from the British Library
ISBN 978-1-7391156-2-3

www.hermits-united.com

Good Beyond Evil

313–238 BC

A radical thinker, Xunzi disagreed with Mencius on human nature. For him men are naturally evil. Starting from this inverse assumption, he yet reached the same Mencian conclusion: moral education is paramount for society to function, and the ruler should be meritorious, protecting the people. This makes Xunzi a Confucianist, though Han Fei and Li Si, his students, were to subvert Confucian principles. From *Xunzi*, Mingyuan Hu selects and translates three treatises illustrating his argument.

人之性惡、其善者偽也 11

Men Are Naturally Evil, 22
Their Goodness
A Matter of Cultivation

人之情乎、人之情乎、甚不美 38

Human Demeanour, 44
All Too Human Demeanour,
Not at All Becoming

水則載舟、水則覆舟 53

Water Carries the Boat; 56
Water Overturns the Boat

人之性悪、其善者偽也

人之性惡、其善者偽也。今人之性、生而有好利焉、順是、故爭奪生而辭讓亡焉。生而有疾惡焉、順是、故殘賊生而忠信亡焉。生而有耳目之欲、有好聲色焉、順是、故淫亂生而禮義文理亡焉。然則從人之性、順人之情、必出於爭奪、合於犯分亂理、而歸於暴。故必將有師法之化、禮義之道、然後出於辭讓、合於文理、而歸於治。用此觀之、人之性惡明矣、其善者偽也。故枸木必將待檃栝烝矯然後直、鈍金必將待礱厲然後利。今人之性惡、必將待師法然後正、得禮義然後治。今人無師法、則偏險而不正。無禮義、則悖亂而不治。古者聖王以人性惡、以為偏險而不正、悖亂而不治、是以為之起禮義、製法度、以矯飾人之情性而正之、以擾化人之情性而導之也、始皆出於治、合於道者也。今人之化師法、積文學、道禮義者為君子。縱性情、安恣孳、而違禮義者為小人。用此觀之、人之性惡明矣、其善者偽也。孟子曰、人之學者、其性善。曰、是不然。是不及知人之性、而不察乎人之性偽之分者也。凡性者、天之就也、不可學、不可事。禮義者、聖人之所生也、人之所學而能、所事而成者也。不可學、不可事、而在人者、謂之性。可學而能、可事而成之在人者、謂之偽。是性偽之分也。今人之性、目可以見、耳可以聽。夫可以見之明不離目、可以聽之聰不離耳、目明而耳聰、不可學明矣。孟子曰、今人之性善、將皆失喪其性故也。
曰、若是則過矣。今人之性、生而
離其樸、離其資、必失而喪之。
用此觀之、然則人之性惡明矣。所
謂性善者、不離其樸而美之、不離
其資而利之也。使夫資樸之於美、
心意之於善、若夫可以見之明不離
目、可以聽之聰不離耳、故曰目明
而耳聰也。今人之性、飢而欲飽、
寒而欲暖、勞而欲休、此人之情性
也。今人見長而不敢先食者、將
有所讓也。勞而不敢求息者、將有

所代也。夫子之讓乎父、弟之讓乎兄、子之代乎父、弟之代乎兄、此二行者、皆反於性而悖於情也。然而孝子之道、禮義之文理也。故順情性則不辭讓矣、辭讓則悖於情性矣。用此觀之、人之性惡明矣、其善者偽也。問者曰、人之性惡、則禮義惡生。應之曰、凡禮義者、是生於聖人之偽、非故生於人之性也。故陶人埏埴而為器、然則器生於陶人之偽、非故生於人之性也。故工人斲木而成器、然則器生於工人之偽、非故生於人之性也。聖人積思慮、習偽故、以生禮義而起法度、然則禮義法度者、是生於聖人之偽、非故生於人之性也。若夫目好色、耳好聽、口好味、心好利、骨體膚理好愉佚、是皆生於人之情性者也。感而自然、不待事而後生之者也。夫感而不能然、必且待事而後然者、謂之生於偽。是性偽之所生、其不同之徵也。故聖人化性而起偽、偽起而生禮義、禮義生而製法度。然則禮義法度者、是聖人之所生也。故聖人之所以同於眾、其不異於眾者、性也。所以異而過眾者、偽也。夫好利而欲得者、此人之情性也。假之有弟兄資財而分者、且順情性、好利而欲得、若是、則兄弟相拂奪矣。且化禮義之文理、若是、則讓乎國人矣。故順情性則弟兄爭矣、化禮義則讓乎國人矣。凡人之欲為善者、為性惡也。夫薄願厚、惡願美、狹願廣、貧願富、賤願貴。苟無之中者、必求於外。故富而不願財、貴而不願

執。苟有之中者、必不及於外。用
此觀之、人之慾為善者、為性惡
也。今人之性、固無禮義、故強學
而求有之也。性不知禮義、故思慮
而求知之也。然則性而已、則人無
禮義、不知禮義。人無禮義則亂、
不知禮義則悖。然則性而已、則悖
亂在已。用此觀之、人之性惡明
矣、其善者偽也。孟子曰、人之性
善。曰、是不然。凡古今天下之所
謂善者、正理平治也。所謂惡者、
偏險悖亂也。是善惡之分也矣。今

誠以人之性固正理平治邪、則有惡用聖王、惡用禮義哉。雖有聖王禮義、將曷加於正理平治也哉。今不然、人之性惡。故古者聖人以人之性惡、以為偏險而不正、悖亂而不治、故為之立君上之執以臨之、明禮義以化之、起法正以治之、重刑罰以禁之、使天下皆出於治、合於善也。是聖王之治而禮義之化也。今嘗試去君上之執、無禮義之化、去法正之治、無刑罰之禁、倚而觀天下民人之相與也。若是、則夫強者害弱而奪之、眾者暴寡而譁之、天下悖亂而相亡、不待頃矣。用此觀之、然則人之性惡明矣、其善者偽也。

Men Are Naturally Evil, Their Goodness A Matter of Cultivation

Men are naturally evil, their goodness a matter of cultivation. People today are inherently profit-driven; following this, contention arises and resignation vanishes. They are intrinsically jealous and malicious; following this, hurt occurs and loyalty dissipates. Their ears and eyes are drawn to pleasure; following this, decadence is bred and propriety wilts. Hence, following human nature, there is contention, decadence and an unholy mess, ending up in violence. Wherefore the teaching of manners and of honour is necessary for civilised conduct conferring to orderly governance. Seen from this, men are clearly evil, their goodness a matter of cultivation.

And so crooked wood must be straightened; blunt metal must be sharpened; men must be educated to be upright and taught propriety to be led. People nowadays are crooked when not educated, ungovernable when not versed in decorum. Ancient sages knew men to be virtueless and lawless; they defined mores and devised laws to shape men's nature and guide their aptitude, so they might be commanded and conform to the Tao. Today, those refined in the letters and acting with rectitude are considered gentlemen; those following their nature and acting unconstrained are considered base. Seen from this, men are clearly evil, their goodness a matter of cultivation.

Mencius said: 'Men learn, as they are good-natured.' I say: Not so. Mencius knows not human nature, and distinguishes not nature from cultivation. Nature is given. It is not learned, cannot be obtained. Propriety being conceived by the sages, men come to it through learning and possess it through practice. That which cannot be learned nor obtained is nature; that which can be learned and practised is cultivation. This is the distinction. Human nature is that which can be seen by the eyes and heard by the ears. Seeing depends on the eyes and hearing depends on the ears. That seeing or hearing is not to be learned is evident.

Mencius said: 'Men are born good. If they do evil, it is not down to their aptitude.' I say: Mencius is mistaken. Men of today part with innocence upon birth; they are sure to lose it.

Seen from this, they are essentially evil, for so-called good nature entails not losing one's innocence, thus embracing beauty; not forsaking one's heart, thus benefiting others. Innocence to beauty and the heart to kindness is like the visible to the eye and the audible to the ear, inseparable. Thence the expression 'clear-sighted and keen-eared', meaning good-natured. But men of today want to be full when hungry; want to be warm when cold; want to rest when tired, such being their aptitude. Now, hungry, they do not eat in the presence of the elderly, giving the latter the food; tired, they do not rest, working in the elderly's place. That a son or a younger brother gives food to his father or elder brother and works in their place goes against his nature. Yet filial piety is the grammar of decorum. Thus, following nature, one does not put the elderly first. That one does so runs counter to nature. Seen from this, men are clearly evil, their goodness a matter of cultivation.

Some ask: 'If men are naturally evil, from where comes propriety?' I answer: From the cultivation of the sages, not from the nature of men. Potters make pots, the pots coming from the cultivation of the potters and not from the nature of men. Carpenters make wares, the wares coming from the cultivation of the carpenters and not from the nature of men. Reflecting deeply on human affairs, the sages conceived decorum and law, decorum and law coming from the cultivation of the sages, not from the nature of men. That the eye is attracted to colour, the ear to music, the tongue to delicacies, the heart to profits and the body to pleasure, is all part of human fallibility, innate and independent of external making. What is not innate and is reliant on efforts is human accomplishment.

This is the distinction between nature and cultivation.

Hence, to refine human nature, the sages cultivate; with cultivation comes decorum; with decorum comes law, decorum and law being of the sages' making. Where the sages differ not from the rest, is their human fallibility; where they differ from and surpass the rest, is their accomplishment. Love for profits is human nature. Following this nature, when profits are to be had, brothers battle over them. Following the grammar of decorum, where profits are at stake, people stand behind their fellow citizens. Thence, by nature, brothers fight one another; following decorum, citizens put others first.

He who yearns to be good is evil by nature. For the meagre yearns for the lavish, the ugly for the pretty, the narrow-minded for the broad-minded, the poor for the rich, and the humble for the noble. What one has not, one seeks out. Ergo, the rich do not wish for fortune, nor the highborn for prestige. What they have, they seek not. Seen from this, he who yearns to be good is evil by nature. Possessing no inborn decorum, men of today learn to acquire it. Knowing no immanent decorum, they ruminate to understand it. Left to nature, men have not and know not decorum. He who has not decorum has chaos. He who knows not decorum knows tumult. Left to nature, tumult springs from within. Seen from this, men are clearly evil, their goodness a matter of cultivation.

Mencius said: 'Men are born good.' I say: Not so. Everywhere, good has meant principle, reason, peace and order; evil has meant bias, imbalance, tumult and chaos. Such is the distinction between good and evil. If human nature were intrinsically principled, reasonable, peaceful and orderly, why need there be sages and kings, propriety and honour? Why would sages, kings, propriety and honour reinforce principle, reason, peace and order? It is simply not so; men are naturally evil. Ancient sages knew men to be evil; they knew them to be biased, unstable, unprincipled; knew them to be confused, disorderly, ungovernable. So they affirmed kingly might to lead, elucidated mores to educate, launched laws to rule, and amplified punition to oust crime, conforming society to the good, such being the governance of sage kings and the instruction of rectitude. Now, if we abolish kingly decree, abandon moral education, annul the rule of law and abate punishment, stand aside and watch how people react: the strong will rob the weak, the many will trample the few, the world will die of chaos and tumult, and all that in no time. Seen from this, men are clearly evil, their goodness a matter of cultivation.

人之情乎、人之情乎、甚不美

堯問於舜曰、人情何如。舜對曰、人情甚不美、又何問焉。妻子具而孝衰於親、嗜慾得而信衰於友、爵祿盈而忠衰於君。人之情乎、人之情乎、甚不美、又何問焉。唯賢者為不然。有聖人之知者、有士君子之知者、有小人之知者、有役夫之知者。多言則文而類、終日議其所以、言之千舉萬變、其統類一也、是聖人之知也。少言則徑而省、論而法、若佚之以繩、是士君子之知也。其言也諂、其行也悖、其舉事多悔、是小人之知也。齊給便敏而無類、雜能旁魄而無用、析速粹孰而不急、不恤是非、不論曲直、以期勝人為意、是役夫之知也。有上勇者、有中勇者、有下勇者。天下有中、敢直其身、先王有道、敢行其意、上不循於亂世之君、下不俗於亂世之民、仁之所在無貧窮、仁之所亡無富貴、天下知之、則欲與天下同苦樂之、天下不知之、則傀然獨立天地之間而不畏、是上勇也。禮恭而意儉、大齊信焉、而輕貨財、賢者敢推而尚之、不肖者敢援而廢之、是中勇也。輕身而重貨、恬禍而廣解苟免、不恤是非然不然之情、以期勝人為意、是下勇也。繁弱、鉅黍、古之良弓也、然而不得排檠則不能自正。桓公之葱、太公之闕、文王之錄、莊君之曶、闔閭之干將、莫邪、巨闕、辟閭、此皆古之良劍也、然而不加砥厲則不能利、不得人力則不能斷。驊騮、騏驥、纖離、綠耳、此皆古之良馬也、然而必前有銜轡

之制、後有鞭策之威、加之以造父
之馭、然後一日而致千里也。夫人
雖有性質美而心辯知、必將求賢師
而事之、擇良友而友之。得賢師而
事之、則所聞者堯舜禹湯之道也。
得良友而友之、則所見者忠信敬讓
之行也。身日進於仁義而不自知也
者、靡使然也。今與不善人處、則
所聞者欺誣詐偽也、所見者污漫淫
邪貪利之行也、身且加於刑戮而不
自知者、靡使然也。傳曰、不知
其子視其友、不知其君視其左右。

靡而已矣。靡而已矣。

Human Demeanour,
All Too Human Demeanour,
Not at All Becoming

Yao asked Shun: 'What is human demeanour?' Shun said: 'Not at all becoming. Why are you even wondering? He who acquires a wife and children, his piety to his parents will wane. His ambition gratified, his loyalty to friends will wane. His function eminent and assets bounteous, his allegiance to the sovereign will wane. Human demeanour, all too human demeanour, not at all becoming. Why are you even wondering? Only honourable men act differently.'

There is the sages' intellect, the gentlemen's intellect, the base men's intellect, and the serf's intellect. Loquacious but composed, reasoning forever upon a principled theme: such is the sages' intellect. Laconic but exact, logical and measured: such is the gentlemen's intellect. Flattering in words, contradictory in deeds, regularly regretting things: such is the base men's intellect. Fast but jumbled, versatile but futile, glib but irrelevant, indifferent to right and wrong and unconcerned by yea or nay, wishing only to outsmart others: such is the serf's intellect.

There is great courage, moderate courage, and lesser courage. Where there is a godly vocation, he defends it; where there is a kingly tradition, he performs it; in troubled times he attends not to the sovereign, nor mingles with the plebeians; goodness being present, he resents not poverty; goodness being absent, he cares not for riches; known by men, he stands with them in sickness and in health; not known, he stands alone on his two own feet, fearless: such is great courage. Courteous and unassuming, he appreciates integrity over material gain, and commends worthy men and discharges the unworthy: such is moderate courage. Appreciating material gain over safety, he shuns not calamity, yet evades responsibility, uncaring of truth or falsity, wishing only to outsmart others: such is lesser courage.

Fan Ruo and Ju Shu were magic bows of antiquity; yet without correction they could not have been aimed. Duke Huan's Cong, Duke Tai's Que, King Wen's Lu, King Zhuang's Hu, King Helü's Gan Jiang, Mo Ye, Ju Que and Pi Lü, were all magic swords of antiquity; yet without being honed they could not have been sharpened, nor cut through anything without the wielding of men. Hua Liu, Qi Ji, Xian Li and Lü Er were all magic horses of antiquity; yet there had to be first bridles and then spurs, not to mention charioteers the likes of Zaofu, for them to run thousands of *li* a day.

Men may be big-hearted and bright; they yet must seek exemplary teachers and befriend kind-hearted friends. Studying under exemplary men, they hear of the virtues of Yao,

Shun, Yu and Tang. Befriending kind-hearted men, they observe acts of loyalty, duty, respect and restraint. Day in and day out, they enter into the realm of goodness and honour without knowing it: such is the force of influence. Now if they take up with the indecorous kind, they will hear of trickery, treachery, dupery and lies, and observe acts of vulgarity, obscenity, vice and greed. They will be threatened with castigation and ruination without the slightest inkling: such is the force of influence. From the books of antiquity: 'Not knowing one's own son, one should inspect his friends. Not knowing one's sovereign, one should inspect his entourage.' All a matter of influence! All a matter of influence!

水則載舟、水則覆舟

馬駭輿、則君子不安輿。庶人駭政、則君子不安位。馬駭輿、則莫若靜之。庶人駭政、則莫若惠之。選賢良、舉篤敬、興孝弟、收孤寡、補貧窮、如是、則庶人安政矣。庶人安政、然後君子安位。傳曰、君者、舟也。庶人者、水也。水則載舟、水則覆舟、此之謂也。故君人者、欲安、則莫若平政愛民矣。欲榮、則莫若隆禮敬士矣。欲立功名、則莫若尚賢使能矣。是君人者之大節也。三節者當、則其餘莫不當矣。三節者不當、則其餘雖曲當、猶將無益也。孔子曰、大節是也、小節是也、上君也。大節是也、小節一出焉、一入焉、中君也。大節非也、小節雖是也、吾無觀其餘矣。

Water Carries the Boat;
Water Overturns the Boat

The horse startled, the gentleman ahorse cannot sit at ease. The people startled, the gentleman on high cannot rule at ease. It is best to calm a startled horse. It is best to content a startled people. Select the worthy and trustworthy, elevate the fair and civil, advocate filial and fraternal piety, foster the orphaned and widowed, and support the poor and impoverished, so people are at ease with politics. When people are at ease with politics, gentlemen are at ease with governance. As stated in the books of antiquity: 'The sovereign resembles the boat; people resemble water. Water carries the boat; water overturns the boat.'

Ergo, for the sovereign to be at ease, he ought to conduct impartial policies and protect the people. To achieve glory, he ought to heed decorum and honour the honourable. To gain success, he ought to laud the laudable and appoint the able. Such are the vital points to governance. These three exercised, all the rest will be in place. These three not in place, nothing else will be.

Confucius said: 'Getting the main points right and likewise the minor ones, he is an exceptional ruler. Getting the main points right and on occasion the minor ones, he is a decent ruler. Getting the main points wrong, even if he gets some minor ones right, he is not worth my attention.'